THE OFFICIAL

MANCHESTER UNITED

ANNUAL 1998

MANCHESTER UNITED
OFFICIAL BOOKS

MADCAP

STICK YOUR PHOTO HERE

First published in 1997 by Manchester United Books/Madcap Books, André Deutsch Ltd, 106 Great Russell Street, London, WC1B 3LJ, England. André Deutsch is a subsidiary of VCI plc.

Text Copyright © 1997 Manchester United Books/Madcap Books Photographs © Action Images/ Allsport/Zone Ltd

A catalogue record for this title is available from the British Library

ISBN 0 233 99164 6

Cover design by Don MacPherson Book design by David Farris

Printed by Mladinska Knjiga Tiskarna, Slovenia

THIS OFFICIAL MANCHESTER UNITED ANNUAL BELONGS TO

School: _____

Date of Birth: _____

My own football team: _____

Position played: _____

My favourite player: _____

TM

SOLO RUN

Today, only the legendary Sir Matt Busby outnumbers Alex Ferguson in the list of trophies won by Manchester United under his management – and like Sir Matt, Alex Ferguson CBE began his playing career in his native Scotland. The future United Manager was born on the last day of 1941 in Govan, Glasgow, where he played for Govan High School, Glasgow Schools and Scotland Schools. After a spell as an amateur with Queen's Park FC, with whom he represented both Scotland Youth and Scotland Amateurs, Alex Ferguson made his League debut in the Scottish Second Division in November 1957.

Three years later he moved to St Johnstone, where he set himself the difficult task of playing part-time football while doing a full-time job. Even so, he scored nineteen goals in his thirty-seven League appearances before joining Dunfermline Athletic in1964 as a full-time professional footballer.

After three successful years with Dunfermline, he moved to Rangers for two and a half years and then joined Falkirk, where he added coaching to his playing duties. In September 1973, Alex Ferguson made his final move as a player, transferring to Ayr United where he played as a part-timer while also running a public house named 'Fergie's Bar'. Alex Ferguson has never been afraid of hard work!

In July 1974, he started work as a football manager, first with East Stirlingshire and then, three months later, with St Mirren. Under his leadership they won the First Division Championship in 1976-7, before further success resulted in the departure of the manager to Aberdeen in 1978.

Over the next eight years Alex Ferguson established himself as one of the top football managers in the country, guiding 'the Dons' to three Premier League titles, four Scottish Cup victories and one League Cup win. In European competition, Aberdeen beat the favourites, Real Madrid to win the European Cup Winners' Cup, in 1983.

In 1986, he stepped into the shoes of Jock Stein to manage Scotland during the World Cup Finals in Mexico. But Alex Ferguson did not wish to take up the job of Scottish manager full-time, nor was he tempted by the other attractive offers that came his way from Scottish and English clubs – that's until the opportunity came to manage Manchester United. Remembering how Jock Stein had always regretted turning down the biggest club in English football, Alex Ferguson accepted and opened another glorious chapter on his already glittering career.

In his first full season as manager, 1987-8, United were runners-up in the League. Two difficult seasons followed and then United started the climb to the top that they have followed ever since. In 1990 they won the FA Cup, defeating Crystal Palace 1-0 after a replay, the following season, Ferguson's team were League Cup runners-up, before defeating Barcelona 2-1 in the European Cup Winners Cup Final.

In 1991-2 United missed out again on the League Championship, which was won by Leeds United, though Ferguson and his players were rewarded by a 1-0 victory over Nottingham Forest which won them the League Cup Final.

It was the arrival of the FA Premier League in 1992-93 that finally brought the League Championship back to Old Trafford, after twenty-six years. For Alex Ferguson, it also brought the trophy of Manager of the Year, which he won the following year when United again won the Championship, making them only the sixth team to win the League

FOCUS ON FERGIE

and Cup double.

Those 1993 victories made Alex Ferguson the first manager to win League titles north and south of the border, as well as being the only man to manage two European Cup Winners' Cup winning sides in different countries.

However, Alex Ferguson knows how to handle set-backs as well as success. Such was the case in the 1995 season when Eric Cantona was given a nine month ban by the FA for kicking an abusive Crystal Palace fan who taunted him after he had been sent off. Without the inspiration of their French star, United failed to clinch any titles and for the first time in five years the club ended the season with no trophies to their credit.

At the start of the 1995-6 season, United took to the field without key players like Mark Hughes, Andrei Kanchelskis and Paul Ince, who had moved to other clubs, and without Cantona, who was still banned. In their place came the string of talented youngsters who were working their way through the highly successful youth system to win first-team places. Led by Cantona, who returned during the season, United stormed to success and by the end of the season clinched a historic 'Double Double', with a team containing five players under twenty-one! Following

on from the disappointments of the previous season, this success confirmed Alex Ferguson as a truly great manager, as his title as Carling Premiership Manager of the Year demonstrated yet again.

In November 1996 he celebrated ten years at Old Trafford, making him the longest serving manager of Manchester United since Sir Matt Busby. The 1996-7 season ended with United collecting their fourth Premiership title and narrowly missing the European Cup Final, after losing to the eventual winners Borussia Dortmund. The season brought justly-earned rewards for the manager, too, who was made Carling Premiership Manager of the Year once again, to crown his ten triumphant years as Manager of Manchester United.

Denis Irwin

Denis Irwin has been a key part of United's defence, ever since he was signed by Alex Ferguson in the summer of 1990. Before then the quiet Irishman had been playing for Oldham Athletic and, before that, for Leeds United.

Denis appeared for Leeds seventy-two times after signing as a sixteen-year-old apprentice. Playing for Oldham, he helped the club reach the 1990 League Cup final and the 1990 FA Cup semi-final against Manchester United. Soon after that Denis Irwin swapped strip, to appear from then on in the colours of Manchester United.

In his first season with United he collected a European Cup Winners' Cup medal. In his second season he helped United win the league Cup for the first time in the club's history, and has since played a vital part in the club's continuing success. This is matched by his regular appearances for the Republic of Ireland, for whom he played in the World Cup Finals in America in 1994.

Born in Cork on 10 October 1971, Roy Keane did not start playing football in England until he was eighteen years old. His footballing career began with Cobh Rangers from whom he transferred to Nottingham Forest after catching the eye of the Forest manager Brian Clough. The fee paid was £10,000 – quite a bargain in comparison with the £3,750,000 that United had to pay for the Irish star, when Alex Ferguson signed him in July 1993. Although Forest were relegated at the end of his second season with the club, Roy Keane's own fortunes fared better. He had already been awarded his full international cap by the Republic of Ireland manager, Jack Charlton, and when he signed for United he set a club and English record for the transfer fee.

A month later he made his debut against Norwich City and has mirrored the club's success since then, taking over as captain from Eric Cantona, when the Frenchman was absent from the team.

Roy Keane

Manchester United spearheaded the entry of English clubs into European competitions when they lined up against Anderlecht of Belgium on 12 September 1956, in the first match of their first European Cup competition. Playing away on that occasion, they won 2-0. But their performance in the home leg just over a fortnight later was spectacular, as United fans were treated to a 10 - 0 victory by Matt Busby's spell-binding team.

Further victories over Borussia Dortmund (does the name ring a bell?) and Athletico Bilbao, set them up for a semi-final clash with the great Spanish side, Real Madrid. After losing 1-3 in the away leg, United could only manage a 2-2 draw at home, giving the Spanish side, who went on to win the competition, victory on aggregate.

The following season brought wins over Shamrock Rovers, Dukla Prague and Red Star Belgrade. Victory over the last of these secured a semi-final meeting with AC Milan, and Matt Busby's team were looking forward to this as they flew home to Manchester. Then tragedy struck when their aircraft crashed at Munich, destroying the hopes and ambitions of the Busby Babes on that cold, bitter night.

As Matt Busby fought his way back to full health, Jimmy Murphy pieced together a side to take on the mighty Italian team. United won 2-1 in the first leg at Old Trafford, but a week later they lost 4-0 and their European dreams were dashed once again.

It was five years before Manchester United again competed in Europe, this time in the Cup Winners' Cup. Tilburg Willem II of Holland and Tottenham Hotspur fell to Matt Busby's men, but the Portuguese champions, Sporting Lisbon, pulled off a stunning 0-5 victory in the away leg in Portugal, which ended United's run that season.

After competing in the Fairs Cup in 1964-5, in which they reached the semi-final, only to be prevented from going further by the Hungarian side, Ferencvaros, United were again in action in the 1965-6 European Cup. In the quarter-finals they came up against the mighty Portuguese side, Benfica – the Eagles of Lisbon.

The Benfica side of the 1960s won almost all the League titles and had already won the European Cup in 1961 and 1962 when they took on United at Old Trafford in the first leg, on 2 February 1966. When the final whistle blew, United had won 3-2. But the away leg, in Benfica's massive home ground, the Stadium of Light which could hold 120,000, was going to require everything Matt Busby's side had to offer. They did not fail their manager. Two goals from George Best and a goal each from Connelly, Crerand and Charlton gave them a 5-1 victory and a semi-final place against Partizan Belgrade.

Unfortunately United failed to score a goal against their Yugoslav opponents in either game. The only goal in their favour was an own goal in the leg played at Old Trafford.

This was the background,

1968 THE EUROPEA

then, to the European Cup challenge they mounted in the 1967-8 season.

Ten years after Munich, Matt Busby had rebuilt a team worthy of the Busby Babes. With the powerful attacking skills of players like Best, Charlton and Law, and a defence that included Crerand, Foulkes and Stiles, hopes were high when United met the Maltese side Hibernians on 20 September 1967, for the first round first leg at Old Trafford. Beating the part-timers from Malta 4-0 made the round look easy. But in the return leg a week later, on a hot, hard, uneven pitch in Malta, Busby's men were hard pushed to hold their opponents to a nil-nil draw.

In the second round, they took on Sarajevo and for the second time in two games had to settle for a 0-0 draw in the first leg. The return leg at Old Trafford was no easier, but goals by Aston and Best gave United victory.

At the end of February 1968 the visitors to Manchester were the Polish champions, Gornik Zabrze. Little was

Bobby Charlton with Sir Matt Busby, Jimmy Murphy (left) and Jack Compton after the semi-final in Madrid

ROAD TO WEMBLEY

known about them, but they proved worthy opposition. Only an own goal separated the teams until the final minute of the match, when Jimmy Ryan put in a shot that Brian Kidd backheeled into the net to give a 2-0 victory.

Kidd's goal turned out to be a life-saver for United. The return leg was played in a Polish snowstorm. Gornik scored the only goal but United managed to scrape through to their fourth semi-final.

Here, they came up against Real Madrid, the victors of the 1957 clash and the team which had dominated the European Cup in its first five years. The first leg at Old Trafford was hard graft for both sides.

Only one goal was scored in the game and, luckily for United, it was George Best who blasted it into the Real net to give the thinnest of leads as they went into the return tie.

That game at Real's magnificent Bernabeu Stadium was watched by 120,000 Spanish fans who were treated to a feast of footballing skills and thrills. After forty minutes the Spanish side were 2-1 up on aggregate. Then Zocco put the ball into his own net. United's spirits were raised, only for Amancio to strike just before the interval. However, Matt Busby told his men that the score was only 3-2 on aggregate

and one more goal would win the tie.

His wise words worked. With only twenty minutes of the game to go, Sadler scored and then Bill Foulkes got the equalizer. Foulkes was the only surviving player in the United team from the side that had been beaten by Real Madrid in 1957. It was a fairy-tale ending to a brilliant game and Manchester United had reached their first European Cup Final. Ahead lay a memorable match at Wembley with their other major European opponents – Benfica.

The Portuguese team were out for revenge for their 5-1 defeat at home two years earlier. They were also in their fifth European Cup Final. United, who had never progressed so far in the competition, were also without Denis Law. Many in the stands feared that his absence might make all the difference to United's hopes. But there were no such fears among the players on the pitch.

The first half passed without a goal to either side. But the game took off after the interval when Sadler's cross found Charlton, who steered the ball into the Benfica net to put United ahead. Benfica responded with a spell of almost unbearable pressure and ten minutes from the end they scored the equalizer, to set the game up for a thrilling finish. Eusebio, Benfica's star player, raced through United's defences twice, only to have both his blistering shots miraculously saved by Alex Stepney in goal.

In extra time, United took control of the game. Soon after play started again, a long clearance by Stepney found Best, who lived up to his name, and produced a

Tonny Dunn, Brian Kidd, Pat Crerand and George Best (on ground) in The European Cup Final against Benfica

dazzling, weaving run that sliced through the Benfica defence and ended with the ball in the back of their net. He was followed a couple of minutes later by Brian Kidd who headed in United's third. Five minutes later Bobby Charlton hammered in his second and United's unbeatable fourth goal. At last the European Cup that Matt Busby had pursued for so many years was on its way to Old Trafford.

Charlton's two goals, Best's brilliant footwork, Kidd's header, Alex Stepney in goal and the likes of Bill Foulkes in defence had overcome the mightiest team in Europe. For all those who had lived through the tragedy of Munich, there could have been no better tribute to their club mates who had perished ten years earlier.

Most fitting of all, perhaps, was that Manchester United, the club that had led English sides into European competition, should be the first to win Europe's greatest prize.

Matt Busby, who could be said to be the founding father of the modern Manchester United, was born ninety-nine years ago, on 26 May 1909, in the Lanarkshire village of Orbiston. After playing for the Ayrshire side, Denny Hibs, he joined Manchester City on 11 February 1928 and made 202 League appearances, mainly at right-half, for the Manchester club.

In March 1936 Busby was transferred to Liverpool for a fee of £8,000, playing there for three years and making 110 League appearances until the outbreak of the Second World War in September 1939. This marked the end of Matt Busby's playing career. During the war he was a PT instructor in the army and had his first taste of football management when he took an Army FA team on a series of exhibition matches to entertain troops in southern Europe. Between 1942 and 1945 Busby also played in seven unofficial international matches against England, in several of which he captained the Scottish team. Earlier in his career, he won one full international cap playing against Wales.

At the end of the war, in 1945, Matt Busby was appointed manager of Manchester United. It was a daunting task. The club owed money to the bank and Old Trafford had been a bomb site for four years. However, Matt Busby rose to the challenge and made the first of his many brilliant signings when he appointed Jimmy Murphy, who had been his opposite number in the 1933 international against Wales, to work alongside him to rebuild the team.

In 1947, 1948 and 1949 United were League runners-up. They won the FA Cup in 1948, were runners-up once more in 1951, and the title flag finally came to Old Trafford in 1952.

By now the club had a well-established youth system that was starting to send a stream of talented young players through to the first team, among them Jeff Whitefoot, Jackie Blanchflower, Roger Byrne, Bill Foulkes, Mark Jones, David Pegg, Liam Whelan, Eddie Colman and Duncan Edwards. The 'Busby Babes' as this new, young side soon became known, won the League in 1956 and 1957 and were FA Cup finalists in 1957.

With domestic success well established, Matt Busby looked beyond home competitions. He wanted to put United at the top of European football and in spite of opposition from the Football League, he took his young side to the semi-finals of the European Cup in 1957, losing to Real Madrid, who went on to win the trophy.

The following season promised to make real Matt Busby's dream, but no one could have imagined the cruel blow that lay in wait for the manager and his team. On the flight home from a European Cup quarter-final fixture against the Yugoslav side Red Star Belgrade, the plane crashed at Munich airport while trying to take off. Eight players, the club Secretary, the trainer and the coach died. Others were seriously injured, including the manager, but his courage saw him through. While Matt Busby recovered, Jimmy Murphy hastily rebuilt a team that heroically reached the FA Cup final, losing 2-0 to Bolton Wanderers.

Over the next ten years Matt Busby strengthened United, building on his previous success and filling the gaps tragically left by the Munich disaster. United legends like Denis Law, Noel Cantwell, Pat Crerand and George Best were signed. In 1963 United claimed the FA Cup. In 1965 they took the Championship, and repeated this success two years later, in 1967. However, the European Cup still beckoned Matt Busby and (as you'll find elsewhere in this book) ten years after the tragedy at Munich he saw his team triumph and bring Europe's leading trophy back to Old Trafford.

This success crowned one of the greatest careers in the history of football. In 1968, Matt Busby was knighted by the Queen and four years later was made a Knight Commander of St Gregory by the Pope. In 1968 he was also named as Manager of the Year. Further distinctions followed after his decision to retire at the end of the 1968-69 season, although he returned briefly to manage the club for the closing months of the following season.

Sir Matt became a director of Manchester United in 1970. Ten years later he became President of the club and in 1982 he was elected Vice-President of the Football League. In 1993, Warwick Road North was renamed Sir Matt Busby Way, a fitting tribute to the man described as 'Mister Manchester United'.

His death, on 20 January 1994, attracted world-wide tributes. Thousands lined the streets of Manchester as he was driven on his final journey to Old Trafford before his burial in the city's Southern Cemetery. Gifts and tributes flocked in from around the country. Thousands of supporters, many from other clubs, sent scarves that created a multi-coloured memorial to this great man, whose bronze statue now stands at the scoreboard end of Old Trafford as an eternal reminder of the proud and determined spirit that still inspires Manchester United today.

FAMOUS FIRSTS

Manchester United were the first English team to win the European Cup.

Manchester United were the first English team to compete in all three major European competitions: European Cup, European Cup-Winners' Cup and European Fairs' Cup/ UEFA Cup.

Manchester United were the first team to score nine goals in an FA Premier League game when they beat Ipswich Town 9–0, on 4 March 1995.

Manchester United were the first team to do the 'Double Double', becoming champions and FA Cup winners in the same season.

Eric Cantona was the first player to score two penalties in an FA Cup Final.

Eric Cantona was the first player to score a hat-trick in the Premier League.

Eric Cantona was the first player born outside the UK to captain an FA Cup winning team, when he led United to victory in the 1995-96 season.

Eric Cantona was the first player ever to win consecutive English League Championship medals with different clubs.

Sir Bobby Charlton was the first footballer to appear on *This is Your Life*.

David Beckham scored his first league goals for Preston, where he played seven games as a loan player.

Manchester United were the first team to win the Premiership title, which they clinched without playing, when Aston Villa lost at home to Oldham Athletic.

During his time with Manchester United, Eric Cantona's strike rate was a goal every other game.

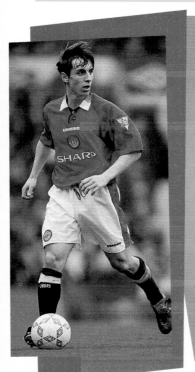

BROTHERS IN ARMS

Currently the Neville brothers, Gary and Phil play for United but . . .

Jimmy and Brian Greenhoff also played for United (most famously, perhaps, in the 1977 FA Cup Final win against Liverpool.

So did Martin and George Buchan.

And Nobby Stiles played for United alongside his brother-in-law, Johnny Giles.

Ryan Giggs

Although Ryan Giggs captained England Schoolboys (because he went to school in England), there is no question that United's star is Welsh at heart.

Ryan was born in Cardiff on 29 November 1973 and moved to live in England when he was seven. There he started playing with Dean's Youth FC and there he was spotted by the club's coach and Manchester City scout, Denis Schofield. It was thanks to him that Ryan Giggs played for the City school of excellence until he was fourteen.

His fourteenth birthday brought an unexpected present from an unexpected visitor. On the day, Alex Ferguson arrived at Ryan's home to ask him to sign schoolboy forms for United. Once Manchester City had confirmed that they would not be signing him, Ryan signed associate schoolboy forms for Manchester United. That was in February 1988. When he was sixteen he signed amateur forms and shortly after his seventeenth birthday, he turned professional.

Four months later Ryan made his professional debut, going on at Old Trafford as a substitute for Denis Irwin in a match against Everton. At the end of that season he made his full first team debut in the Manchester Derby, and rounded it off by scoring the only goal of the game.

After an injury to Lee Sharpe at the start of the 1991-2 season enabled him to take over on the United left-wing, Ryan Giggs has gone from strength to strength. With Manchester United he has won every domestic trophy: the League Cup (1992), four League Championships (1993, 1994, 1996 and 1997), two FA Cup winners' medals (1994 and 1996) and a runners-up medal in 1995. As if that record was not enough, Ryan Giggs is also a key member of the Welsh national team.

JIGSAW PUZZLE

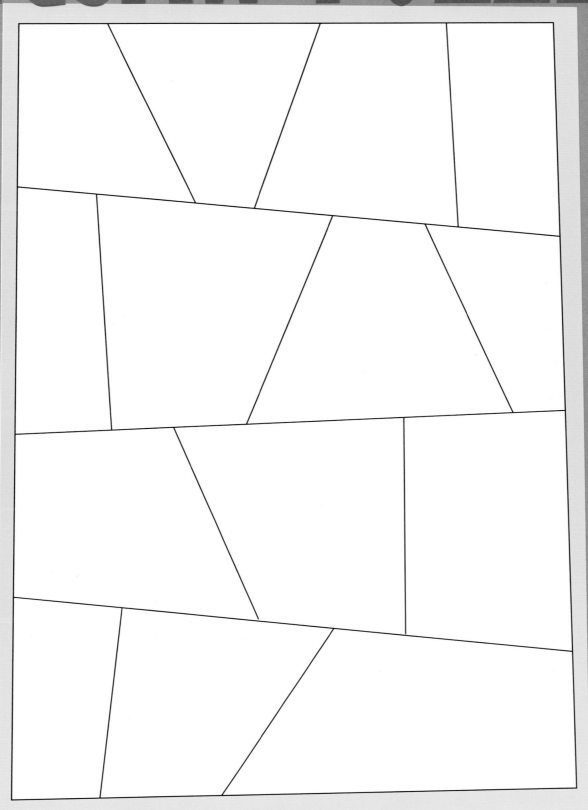

Cut out the shapes on this page and fit them into the empty grid opposite to discover some dramatic football action!

(Why not photocopy this page and cut that up?)

(The whole picture is on the last page)

Fan...tastic poems!

Every week the Junior Views office at Manchester United receive poems from young fans. Here are two about the club written by ten year olds Mark and Lindsey.

Man U

Hi, I'm ten and my name is Mark, the nearest ground to me is
Blundell Park.
My Dad got some tickets to see Man United - he asked me to come
I was very excited,
I love Man United they're my favourite team - especially Ryan
Giggs, he plays like a dream.
We left Grimsby Town at around 12 noon, I felt so happy we'd be at
Old Trafford soon.
When we arrived at about 2 o'clock, I did not realise I'd be in for a shock.
My visions of Old Trafford were way off the mark - just a little bit different from Blundell Park,
I looked on in awe, sat glued to my seat, when Giggsy ran out with
a ball at his feet.
The game got started and - Oh! What a pity, the first goal was scored by Manchester City,
Half-time approached and I felt a bit sad. 'Cheer up, we'll thrash 'em' chirped in my Dad.
Giggsy took a corner, Cantona got pushed. The Frenchman took the corner not even getting flushed.
One-all the score, I'm as tense as can be. What a fantastic game -
I'm glad I'm me.
10 minutes to go. Will the score stay the same? Will they score? Won't they score? It's hurting my brain.
Cantona to Giggs, Giggs makes a pass. It's in the back of the net -
there's uproar in the park.
I jumped off my seat, punched my arms to the sky. 'We've won! We've won!' I started to cry.
The final whistle blew. It's the end of the game. I'm sorry Giggs didn't score, but I'm glad I came.
Back to the car for my Dad and me.
One of the best days of my life.
Now it's back home for tea.

Mark Collins (aged 10)
Cleethorpes,
Lincolnshire

MUFC

Manchester United Football Club.
Alex Ferguson is Man United's manager.
Never before has there been a better football team.
Cole will show you how to play football.
Here we go! Here we go! Here we go!
Everyone loves them.
Simply the Best.
The red devils.
Eric Cantona never to be forgotten.
Ryan Giggs is a brilliant football player.

Umbro sponsor the family stand.
Neville is a good player of Man United.
Irwin plays for Man United.
There will never be a better football team.
Everyone knows who Man United are.
David Beckham plays well for Man United.

Lindsey Salisbury (aged 10)
Kempston,
Bedford

Paul Scholes

Paul Scholes was born on 16 November 1974, in Salford. In spite of supporting Oldham Athletic as a lad, he joined United on trainee forms in July 1991 and turned professional eighteen months later in January 1993. Paul showed early signs of his footballing promise. In 1992 he won an FA Youth Cup winners' medal, followed by a runners-up medal a year later. In 1993 he was also a member of the England Under-18 team which won the European Championships. But his League debut for United was even more impressive, when he took to the field against Ipswich Town on 24 September 1994 and scored twice in a 3-2 defeat.

Referred to by his manager, Alex Ferguson, as the 'new Eric Cantona', Paul Scholes became a regular first team player during Cantona's suspension in the 1994–5 season, which ended with the club failing to collect any trophies for the first time in five seasons. The following season ended better, with United picking up their third Premier League title in four years, and Paul Scholes his first major honour.

Success has followed him into the international arena. After making his England debut in a match against South Africa, played on his home ground at Old Trafford, Paul made his full international debut against Italy in which he scored in England's 2-0 victory and was voted man of the match.

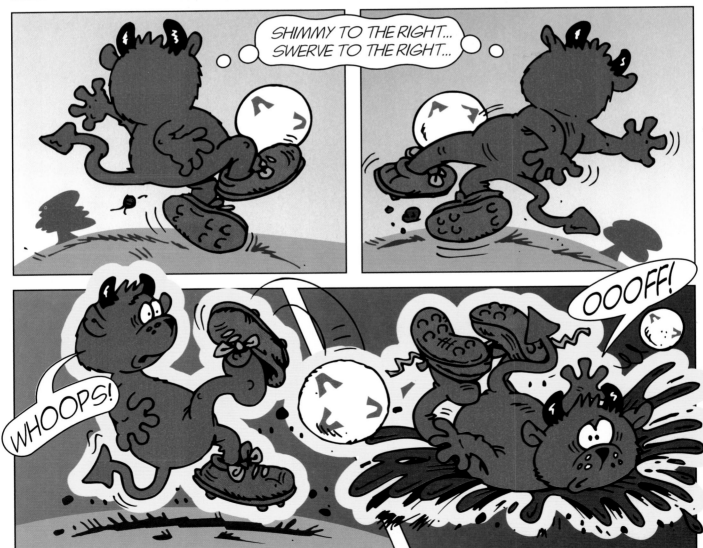

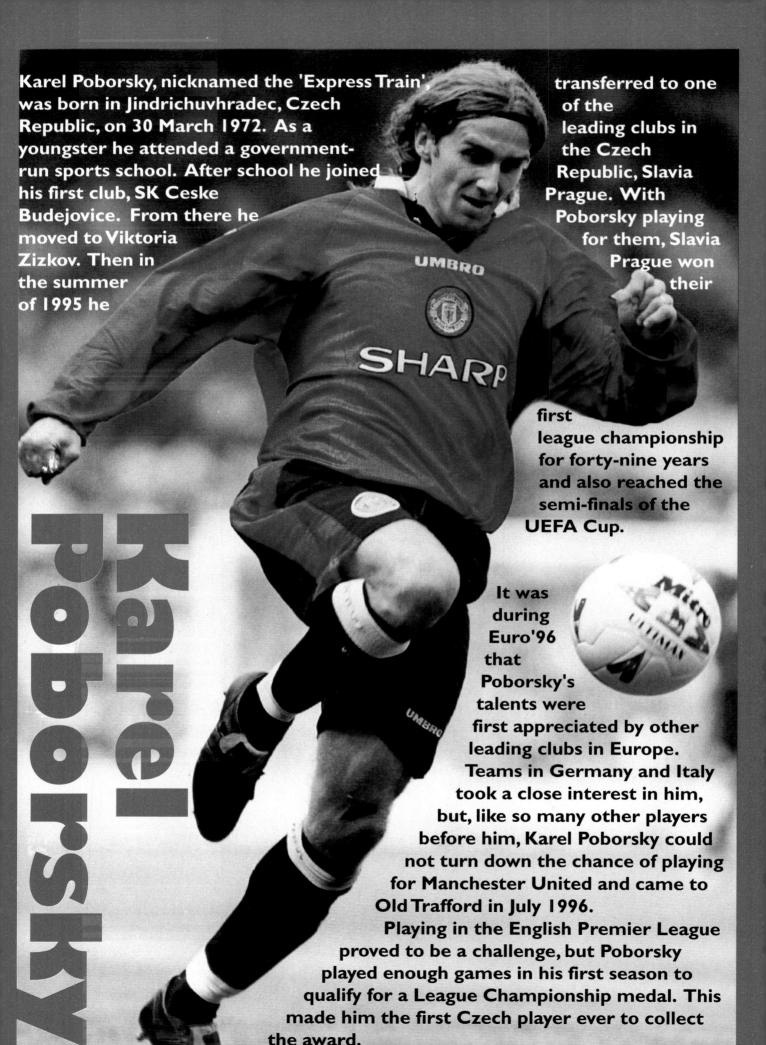

Karel Poborsky, nicknamed the 'Express Train', was born in Jindrichuvhradec, Czech Republic, on 30 March 1972. As a youngster he attended a government-run sports school. After school he joined his first club, SK Ceske Budejovice. From there he moved to Viktoria Zizkov. Then in the summer of 1995 he transferred to one of the leading clubs in the Czech Republic, Slavia Prague. With Poborsky playing for them, Slavia Prague won their first league championship for forty-nine years and also reached the semi-finals of the UEFA Cup.

It was during Euro'96 that Poborsky's talents were first appreciated by other leading clubs in Europe. Teams in Germany and Italy took a close interest in him, but, like so many other players before him, Karel Poborsky could not turn down the chance of playing for Manchester United and came to Old Trafford in July 1996.

Playing in the English Premier League proved to be a challenge, but Poborsky played enough games in his first season to qualify for a League Championship medal. This made him the first Czech player ever to collect the award.

Karel Poborsky

OLD TRAFFORD

THE THEATRE OF DREAMS

'The theatre of dreams'. That's what Bobby Charlton called the stadium that saw some of his greatest appearances on the football field.   But the 'dreams' began long before Robert Charlton was born in Ashington, Northumberland on 11 October 1937.

United became Football League champions for the first time ninety years ago, in 1908 and a year later they followed this by winning the FA Cup for the first time – Manchester United had arrived!

It was decided that a great team needed a great stadium. In those early days United were playing in north Manchester, but in 1909 the club bought land near Trafford Park and set about building the new stadium that was to become Old Trafford.

On 19 February 1910, over 45,000 spectators watched the first game at Old Trafford and saw Liverpool beat United 4-3. A year later though, United were champions again.

At this time it wasn't just United fans who packed the place. As one of the finest football grounds in the country, Old Trafford could hold a crowd of 80,000. The FA used the stadium to stage a Cup Final replay and in 1915 chose Old Trafford for the Cup Final itself. That game, in which Sheffield United beat Chelsea, became known as the 'Khaki' Cup Final because of the thousands of soldiers who watched the game while they were on leave from fighting in the First World War. Apart from cover being added to the 'Popular Terrace' along United Road, Old Trafford remained unchanged between the First World War and the Second World War. The FA Cup semi-final between Wolves and Grimsby on 25 March 1939 drew a record of 76,962 to Old Trafford. But war broke out six months later and on 11 March 1941 United's great ground suffered serious damage during an air-raid. The Main Stand was destroyed by a fire that left it a burnt-out shell. The covered terrace was badly damaged and the pitch was scorched by explosions. It was to be eight years before Manchester United next played at their home ground. In the meantime, the club shared the ground of their local rivals, Manchester City, at Maine Road.

Theatre of Dreams

By the 1949 season Old Trafford was ready to receive players and fans once again and the first game after the war kicked off on 24 August 1949, when Bolton Wanderers were the visitors.

Over the years that followed the club's growing success saw steady changes and improvements. In 1957 floodlights were erected so that mid-week evening European games could be held at Old Trafford. In 1965 a new, enlarged stand was completed along United Road, including the first private boxes at a British football ground. These developments made Old Trafford an automatic choice to host three games in the 1966 World Cup Finals.

The ground continued to be the leading football venue in England outside Wembley when, in 1970, Chelsea won an FA Cup Final replay there, followed by both Aston Villa and Nottingham Forest winning League Cup replays at the 'Theatre of Dreams'.

So great was the pulling power of Old Trafford that in 1986 a different sport altogether, rugby league, decided to show itself off there, when Great Britain played a Test match against Australia. Needless to say, the event attracted a record attendance and since then several other big rugby league games have been staged at United's home ground.

Old Trafford became an all-seater stadium in 1994, with a capacity of 44,000. Such was the demand for tickets for United's home games, however, the ground was extended. In 1995 the North Stand was demolished and replaced with a three-tier one capable of holding 26,000 spectators. When this magnificent new stand was completed, in April 1996, it took Old Trafford's capacity to 55,000, making it the largest stadium in the Premier League.

In this 'premier' position, football 'came home' in Euro 96 when not only group games, but quarter-finals and a semi-final graced United's stadium. In fact football stayed home in 1997, when England played South Africa at Old Trafford in a friendly international.

As premiership after premiership arrives, so Old Trafford continues to fulfil our dreams. As Jordi Cruyff's father, Johan, said, 'If you can't play football here, you can't play it anywhere.'

United's towering goalkeeper was a Manchester United fan even as a youngster growing up in Denmark, where he was born on 18 November 1963 and where he started his playing career.

Playing for Brondby, one of Denmark's top clubs, he won three league titles and was voted Danish Footballer of the Year in 1990.

In spite of this, Peter Schmeichel was still little known when Alex Ferguson signed him in August 1991. However, it took only a few games for United fans to appreciate the manager's judgement. For his first four games the new Danish goalkeeper kept a clean sheet and was soon being hailed as the best United keeper since Alex Stepney.

Schmeichel's first season continued in the same way – in forty-two games he let in just thirty-three goals. It is understandable then, that he was once voted the Best Keeper in the world and that he became a national hero in Denmark after his performance in the 1992 European Championship final.

Peter Schmeichel's talents are not restricted to defence. His long throws spearhead many United attacks and occasionally he joins in with corners, even scoring on one occasion in September 1995 when United played Volgograd.

Peter Schmeichel

Team Game

All the names of players in the Manchester United squad listed below can be found in the grids below and opposite.
All except one name are on two lines, and they may read across, up, down or diagonally, either forwards or backwards.
All the names are in straight lines. You have to work out which names are in which grid, but no names are divided between the two grids.

DAVID MAY

PETER SCHMEICHEL

RAI VAN DER GOUW (4 lines)

NICKY BUTT

DENIS IRWIN

PAUL SCHOLES

OLE SOLSKJAER

KAREL POBORSKY

RONNY JOHNSEN

JORDI CRUYFF

PHIL NEVILLE

ANDY COLE

GARY NEVILLE

CHRIS CASPER

BRIAN McCLAIR

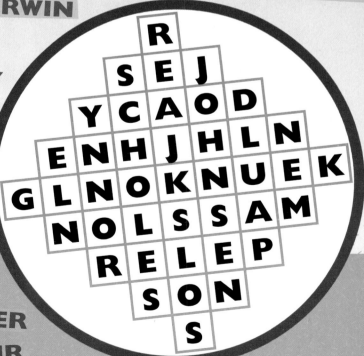

```
            R
         S  E  J
      Y  C  A  O  D
   E  N  H  J  H  L  N
   L  N  O  K  N  U  E  K
G  L  N  O  L  S  S  A  M
N  O  L  S  L  E  P
R  E  L  E  P
S  O  N
      S
```

Design and colour in your own home strip

David Beckham

Although David Beckham was born in Leytonstone, on 2 May 1975, his interest in Manchester United started at an early age. His parents are United supporters and when David was twelve he won a Bobby Charlton Soccer Skills award and received this at Old Trafford on a match day.

At school, David represented Essex Schools. He had trials with Leyton Orient and attended Tottenham Hotspur's school of excellence before signing for Manchester United as a trainee in 1991.

In the following season he made his first team debut, coming on as a substitute for the closing twenty minutes of a League Cup second round tie at Brighton and Hove Albion, on 1 October 1992. His League debut followed on 2 April 1995, playing at home against Leeds United.

As a member of Manchester United's brilliantly successful FA Youth Cup team, he gained a winners' medal in 1992 and a runners-up medal the following season. In 1994 Beckham played sixteen games for the reserves .

With this training and success behind him, David Beckham was well set for the 1995-6 double-winning season, during which he established himself as a worthy replacement for key midfield players like Andrei Kanchelskis and Paul Ince. As a goal-scorer he was soon a household name, with the winning goal of the FA Cup semi-final against Chelsea to his credit and the never-to-be-forgotten goal he scored against Wimbledon from the half-way line on the first game of the season.

In the 1996-7 season David Beckham's success continued at club and international level. As well as helping United to a European Cup semi-final and another Premier League Championship, he won the PFA Young Player of the Year award and came second in the PFA Player of the Year.

Having played for England at Youth and Under-21 levels, he made his first full England debut on 1 September 1996. This selection must have been especially rewarding for the young United star, since the England manager, Glenn Hoddle, had been one of his idols as a youngster.

Odd balls

When Manchester United began playing in Europe, they played early home games at Maine Road, because the Old Trafford flood lights were not ready in time.

England stars David Platt and Peter Beardsley both spent a season with Manchester United, but neither played a League game.

Manchester United are the only British team to have had three different players named European Footballer of the Year: Denis Law, George Best and Bobby Charlton.

Manchester United are the only team to have won the FA Cup at Wembley by four goals to nil - a feat they have achieved twice.

When Manchester United won the FA Cup in 1948, they beat fellow First Division opponents in every round.

Manchester United have won more Premiership games than any other team.

Karel Poborsky scored at Old Trafford before he ever signed for Manchester United. He scored there for the Czech Republic in Euro 96.

Although capped for Wales at senior level, Ryan Giggs has played for England Schoolboys.

In the 1973-74 season Alex Stepney became United's penalty taker and at one point was top scorer with two goals. That may not sound out of the ordinary, except that Alex Stepney was the Manchester United goalkeeper!

Mark the Man

There's the surname of a United player hidden inside each of these sentences. Look carefully and see if you can spot who they are.

a   Who's in a fair wind for France?
b   Who's in ten evil letters?
c   Bob utters kind words.
d   Make an everlasting wish.
e   A song Beck hammers up the charts.
f   Who saw Grandma yesterday?
g   Uncle John sent a letter.

M is for Muddle

Can you sort out this Manchester United mix up? Who got their first caps against whom? Below we have listed three United stars who got their first caps against teams beginning with the letter M. See if you can you match the player to the country he played against.

Denis Irwin ——— Mexico
David Beckham —✕— Moldova
Nicky Butt ——— Morocco

All Change

The names of eight United stars have been changed around in these questions. Can you work out who they are?

a   Who is mixed up in the All Shoes Cup?
b   Who can become Senor Johnny N? *Ronny Johnsen*
c   Who can be changed around to become Mick Baddhave?
d   Who is it that 'wins in ride'?
e   Who lives in Cody Lane?
f   Who becomes Gary Gings? *Ryan Giggs*
g   Which United favourite would never put up with Vera Yelling? *Steve Bruce*
h   Who makes Bunty tick?

In the Middle

Here are six United players and six names (OK, five names, because one name is repeated twice). Each name is the middle name of one of the players. The question is, do you know which name belongs to which player?

Andy Cole   Joseph
Gary Pallister   Alexander
Ryan Giggs   Boleslaw
Denis Irwin   John
Brian McClair   Andrew
Peter Schmeichel   Joseph

You will find all the answers at the back of the book.

on the ball

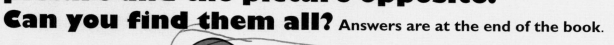

There are eleven differences between this picture and the picture opposite. Can you find them all? Answers are at the end of the book.

Andy Cole

Andy Cole, who was born in Nottingham on 15 October 1971, was marked out for football greatness after playing at Lilleshaw school of excellence and joining Arsenal on schoolboy forms. Playing for England Schoolboys, he scored on his debut, in a 2-0 victory over West Germany.

When his time with Arsenal produced only a limited number of appearances in the first team, he was loaned to Fulham and then Bristol City. There, Andy met with greater success. Bristol City were so impressed by the young forward that in July 1992 they paid Arsenal a club record transfer fee of £500,000. Less than a year later Cole set another club record at Bristol City, when Newcastle paid £1,750,000 for his talents.

This turned out to be money very well spent. In his first season at Newcastle, Andy Cole helped them win promotion to the Premier League. In the following season he scored thirty-four league goals, which earned him the European Golden Boot award and the 1994 PFA Young Player of the Year.

Andy Cole's move to Manchester United in January 1995 set another transfer fee record, when Alex Ferguson paid £6,250,000 (then a British record) to bring him to Old Trafford. In his first season with his new club, Andy scored twelve goals in seventeen games – five of them coming in one game as United defeated Ipswich Town 9-0.

The following season he collected a Premier League Championship medal, having scored one of the goals in United's 3-0 victory at Middlesborough in the last game of the season. Illness, injury and Ole Gunnar Solskjaer's run of goals at the beginning of the next season gave Andy Cole a difficult start, but that season ended on a much happier note as United picked up their fourth League Championship in five years (Andy Cole's second) and he was recalled to the England team after an absence of two years.

Fan...tastic Art!

You've read the poems - here are four pictures sent to the club by the fans.

Jack Meredith

Lyndsey Duckworth aged 12

Monique Chew aged 10

Nana Dabo

Nicky Butt

When Bryan Robson left Manchester United for Middlesborough, he singled out Nicky Butt as a star of the future and he was not to be disappointed. By the time he was twenty-two Nicky Butt had played for England at Schoolboy, Youth, Under-21 and full international level. He also had two Premier League Championship medals, an FA Cup Final winners' medal (and a losers'), a Youth Cup Final medal and a Central League (reserve team) Championship medal.

Born in Manchester on 21 January 1975, he played for Oldham and Greater Manchester Schoolboys, before joining United as a trainee in July 1991. Eighteen months later he turned professional and made his first team debut on 21 November 1992, as a substitute for Paul Ince. As one of Fergie's Fledglings he was the first, apart from Ryan Giggs, to break through to the first team.

Design and colour in your own away strip

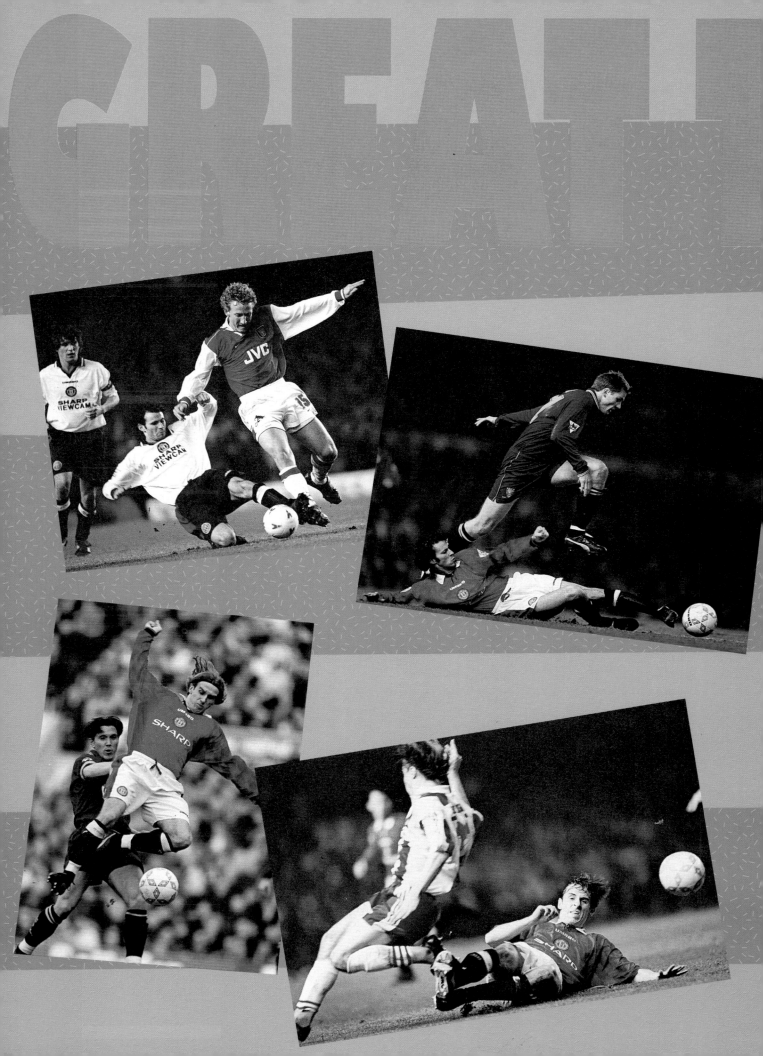

GREAT

You can find all the great names associated with Manchester United
which are listed below in the grid opposite.
The names read in a continuous line, going up and down,
forwards and backwards, but not diagonally.
All the squares in the grid are used; each is used once only.

RON ATKINSON

BILL FOULKES

GEORGE BEST

HARRY GREGG

STEVE BRUCE

GORDON HILL

MATT BUSBY

DENIS LAW

MARTIN BUCHAN

PAUL McGRATH

NOEL CANTWELL

BILLY MEREDITH

BOBBY CHARLTON

BRYAN ROBSON

PADDY CRERAND

NOBBY STILES

TOMMY DOCHERTY

RYAN GIGGS

MARTIN EDWARDS

DENNIS VIOLLET

NORMAN WHITESIDE

ALEX FERGUSON

RAY WOOD

S	O	O	B	S	T	E	S	D	E	N	G	E
B	N	N	B	Y	I	L	I	N	N	O	R	O
O	R	O	N	T	L	O	S	I	N	S	G	E
A	N	R	M	E	L	I	V	K	T	S	T	B
Y	R	N	A	R	O	N	A	T	E	V	S	E
H	B	W	D	E	R	S	U	B	T	E	N	O
T	I	H	I	D	A	B	M	A	T	B	N	E
E	D	I	S	O	Y	Y	E	C	U	R	A	L
R	E	T	E	O	W	M	A	R	N	B	H	C
Y	M	B	H	R	G	Y	D	T	I	U	C	A
L	L	I	T	A	C	C	D	A	L	R	A	N
I	L	I	S	L	M	R	E	P	T	C	H	T
H	L	N	L	U	A	A	R	N	O	Y	E	W
N	D	E	A	W	P	N	D	T	O	B	L	L
O	D	R	O	E	F	X	E	L	M	B	O	B
E	G	G	G	R	G	U	S	A	M	Y	D	O
R	G	Y	R	N	O	S	D	E	N	M	Y	C
S	H	A	R	B	I	L	R	D	I	A	T	H
E	K	L	U	O	F	L	A	W	T	R	R	E

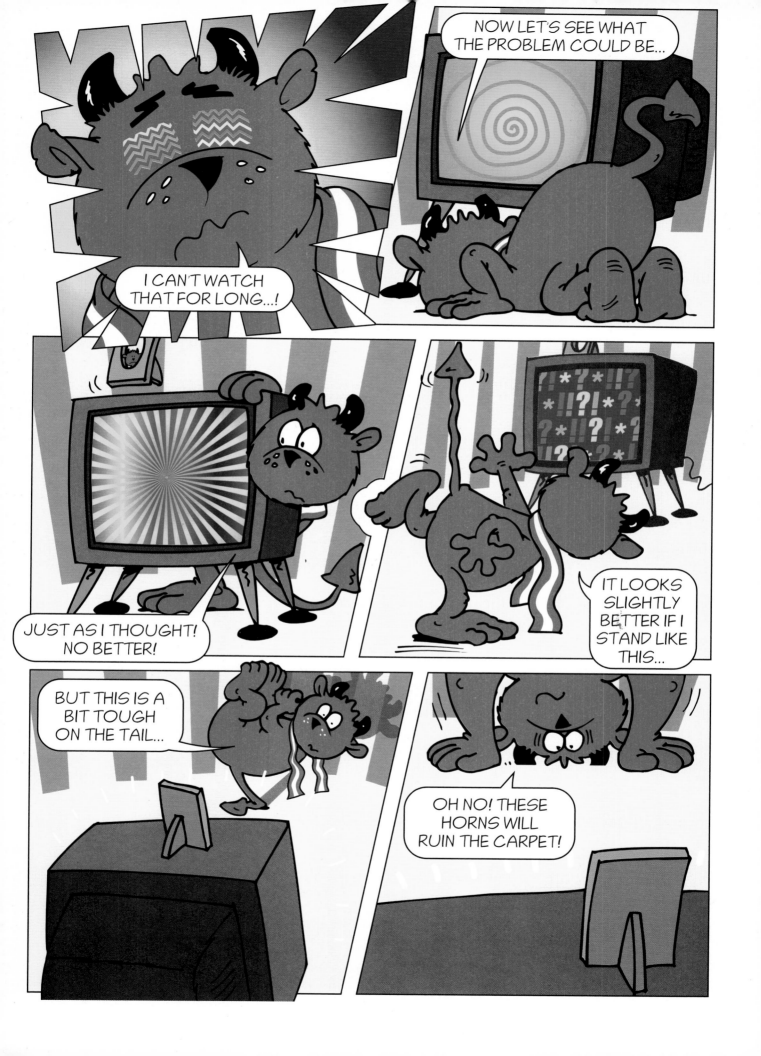

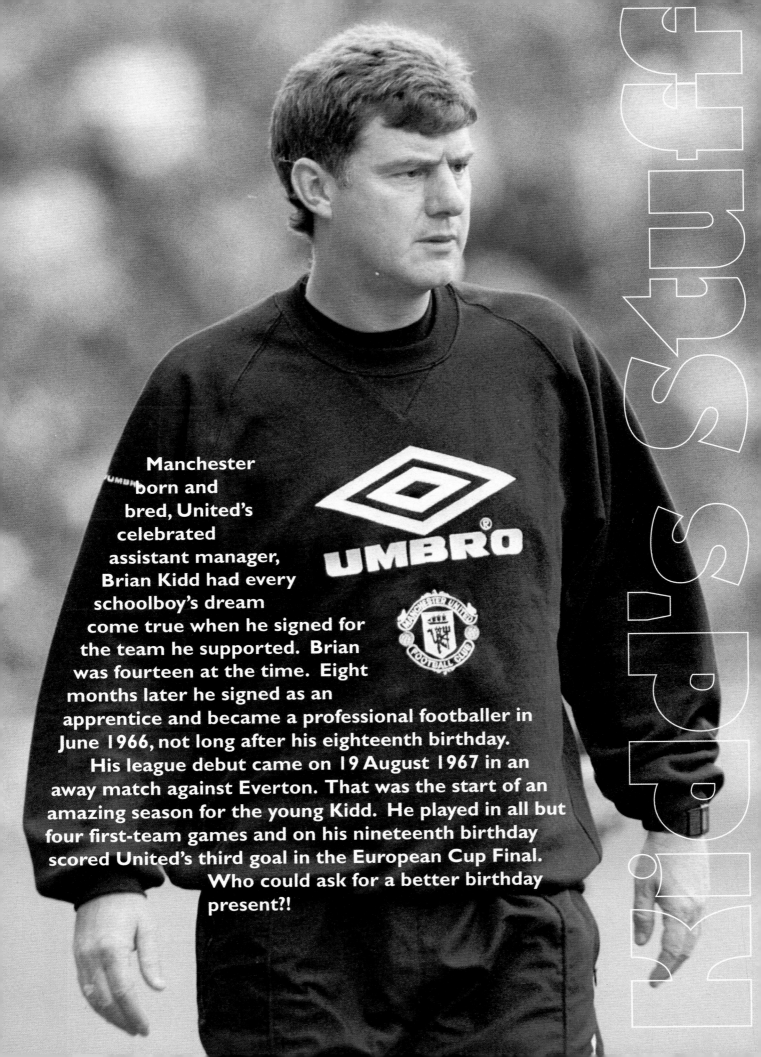

Manchester born and bred, United's celebrated assistant manager, Brian Kidd had every schoolboy's dream come true when he signed for the team he supported. Brian was fourteen at the time. Eight months later he signed as an apprentice and became a professional footballer in June 1966, not long after his eighteenth birthday.

His league debut came on 19 August 1967 in an away match against Everton. That was the start of an amazing season for the young Kidd. He played in all but four first-team games and on his nineteenth birthday scored United's third goal in the European Cup Final. Who could ask for a better birthday present?!

Kidd's Press

From United, Brian Kidd moved to Arsenal in 1974, where he played for two years before returning to his home town to join Manchester City. Everton and Bolton Wanderers also called on his services before he moved to America, where he spent four years as a player. The America's featured significantly in Brian's playing career. He won his first England cap five days before his twenty-first birthday in a match against a team from the South American country of Ecuador.

At the end of his playing career Brian Kidd began a new career in football management, beginning with Barrow in 1984. But Manchester beckoned him once again and four years later he was appointed youth coach at Old Trafford. For many fans, a large part of United's success since that time is thanks to Brian Kidd. His partnership with Alex Ferguson is the most successful at Old Trafford since the days of Matt Busby and Jimmy Murphy.

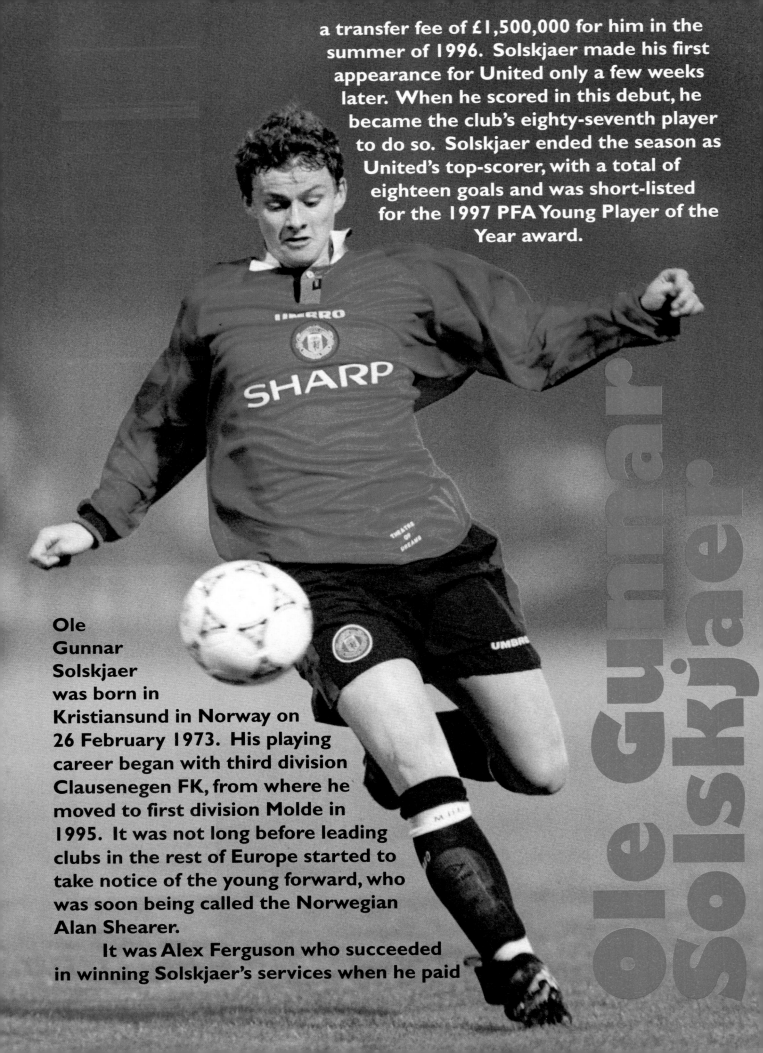

a transfer fee of £1,500,000 for him in the summer of 1996. Solskjaer made his first appearance for United only a few weeks later. When he scored in this debut, he became the club's eighty-seventh player to do so. Solskjaer ended the season as United's top-scorer, with a total of eighteen goals and was short-listed for the 1997 PFA Young Player of the Year award.

Ole Gunnar Solskjaer was born in Kristiansund in Norway on 26 February 1973. His playing career began with third division Clausenegen FK, from where he moved to first division Molde in 1995. It was not long before leading clubs in the rest of Europe started to take notice of the young forward, who was soon being called the Norwegian Alan Shearer.

It was Alex Ferguson who succeeded in winning Solskjaer's services when he paid

Ole Gunnar Solskjaer

Gary Pallister

Born in Ramsgate in 1965, Gary Pallister began his playing career with non-League Billingham Town and stayed there until he was spotted by Middlesbrough Football Club and signed for them. Gary was twenty-one at the time. The following year he was loaned to Darlington, who desperately wanted to hang on to the young defender. However, Darlington could not raise the £4000 transfer fee.

So Gary returned to Middlesbrough and for four years played for the club he had supported as a youngster.

When he did transfer in August 1989, it was for a lot more than £4000! Manchester United paid £2,300,000 for his services, which was then a record fee - but, as so often, it turned out to be money very well spent.

The arrival of Gary Pallister came at the same time that United began one of its most successful runs of all time - and this is probably no coincidence. He has won a major trophy with the club in every season, but 1994-5. He has played for England under four different managers: Bobby Robson, Graham Taylor, Terry Venables and Glenn Hoddle. And in 1992 Gary Pallister was voted PFA Player of the Year.

See how good you are at solving clues with this mega puzzle.
The numbers in brackets show the number
of letters in each word.

Across

6	In your opponents' half of the pitch, and closer to your opponents' goal than the ball (7)
7	What soccer is played with (4)
10	Name of London team known as the 'Gunners' (7)
11	The opposite of 'attack' (7)
12	It's worn on the head (3)
13	Fill in the missing word: 'Kick --- ball!' (3)
15	See 35 Across
19	Manchester United's ground (3, 8)
22	The -------- room is where players change their clothes (8)
27	See 26 Down
28	The referee blows it (7)
30	Middle (6)
31	What the referee needs to do with his eyes (4)
33	If you win, you might get one (5)
34	To do this is the goalkeeper's job (4)
35	and 15 Across Manchester United's number 10 (5, 7)
36	------ Road is Leeds United's ground (6)

Down

1	He umpires the game (7)
2	To try to get the ball from your opponent (6)
3	A free kick might be this or indirect (6)
4	If the ball goes into it a goal is scored (3)
5	One player ------ the ball to another (6)
8	Bramall ---- is Sheffield United's home ground (4)
9	The rectangle in front of the goal (7, 4)
10	A large sports ground (5)
14	A ball hit with your head (6)
15	You wear them on your feet (5)
16	All your soccer clothes make up your --- (3)
18	If the ball goes over one of these it's out of play (9)
20	To run with the ball close to your feet (7)
21	When a player breaks the rules on the pitch it's called a ---- (4)
23	He tries to stop the opposing team from scoring (10)
24	This is what 23 Down tries to do! (5)
25	London club known as the 'Blues' (7)
26,	and 27 Across Name of a Birmingham team (5, 5)
29	Attempt to score a goal (6)
32	First name of Newcastle's Mr Shearer (4)

Crazy Questions

a Who was 24 in 1996 but 10 in 1997? *Beckham*

b Who shares his nickname with a large hunting dog?

c Who are United's two 'corkers'?

Irwin and Keane

(Answers at the back of the book)

...and finally...

Bryan Robson's final goal for United came in United's final game of the 1992-3 season, when he scored against Wimbledon.

Four years later, Bryan was on the receiving end when Gary Neville finally scored for United in the league meeting with Middlesborough at the end of the 1996-7 season. That goal helped United to win the title, but also helped to send Middlesborough down.

Answers

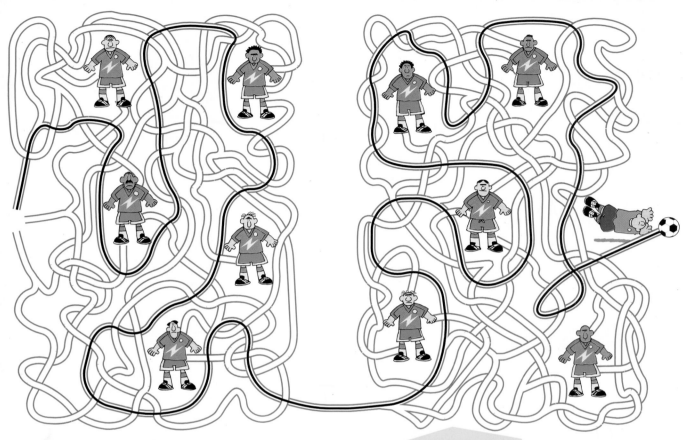

Solo Run Maze

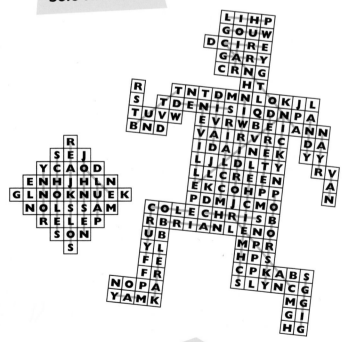

Team Game

Jigsaw

more answers...

Spot the difference

Great Names

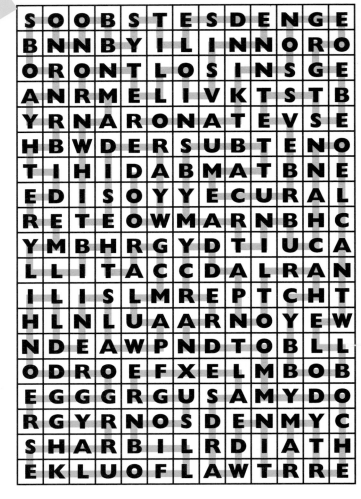

S	O	O	B	S	T	E	S	D	E	N	G	E
B	N	N	B	Y	I	L	I	N	N	O	R	O
O	R	O	N	T	L	O	S	I	N	S	G	E
A	N	R	M	E	L	I	V	K	T	S	T	B
Y	R	N	A	R	O	N	A	T	E	V	S	E
H	B	W	D	E	R	S	U	B	T	E	N	O
T	I	H	I	D	A	B	M	A	T	B	N	E
E	D	I	S	O	Y	Y	E	C	U	R	A	L
R	E	T	E	O	W	M	A	R	N	B	H	C
Y	M	B	H	R	G	Y	D	T	I	U	C	A
L	L	I	T	A	C	C	D	A	L	R	A	N
I	L	I	S	L	M	R	E	P	T	C	H	T
H	L	N	L	U	A	A	R	N	O	Y	E	W
N	D	E	A	W	P	N	D	T	O	B	L	L
O	D	R	O	E	F	X	E	L	M	B	O	B
E	G	G	G	R	G	U	S	A	M	Y	D	O
R	G	Y	R	N	O	S	D	E	N	M	Y	C
S	H	A	R	B	I	L	R	D	I	A	T	H
E	K	L	U	O	F	L	A	W	T	R	R	E

Giant Crossword

On the Ball answers

Mark the Man
a Irwin
b Neville
c Butt
d Keane
e Beckham
f May
g Johnsen

M is for Muddle
Denis Irwin v Morocco
David Beckham v Moldova
Nicky Butt v Mexico

Crazy Questions
a
David Beckham – his squad
shirt number changed
b
Peter Schmeichel – the Great
Dane
c
Denis Irwin and Roy Keane –
both were born in Cork

All Change
a Paul Scholes
b Ronny Johnsen
c David Beckham
d Denis Irwin
e Andy Cole
f Ryan Giggs
g Gary Neville
h Nicky Butt

In the Middle
Andy Alexander Cole
Gary Andrew Pallister
Ryan Joseph Giggs
Peter Boleslaw Schmeichel
Denis Joseph Irwin
Brian John McClair

The publishers would like to thank Zone Ltd for their help in providing the
photographs in this book.
The publishers would also like to thank the Manchester United Museum, in
particular to Zoe Makinson, for the great help given in providing information
on Manchester United past and present. Mike Maxfield and his staff who run
Junior Views at Manchester United also kindly provided the artwork and
poems sent in to them by young fans.